© 2001 by Barbour Publishing, Inc.

ISBN 1-58660-249-7

Cover art © Eyewire

All Scripture quotations are taken from the King James Version of the Bible.

Published by Barbour Books, an imprint of Barbour Publishing, Inc., P.O. Box 719, Uhrichsville, Ohio 44683
www.barbourbooks.com

Printed in China.
5 4 3

Joy to the World

COLLEEN REECE AND
JULIE REECE-DEMARCO

Joy to the World, the Lord Is Come!

There is something about Christmas that brings light and joy into even the darkest hearts. Many things make the holidays special: children's shining eyes, grandparents' memories, bells, holly, carols, manger scenes, and Christmas programs. A spirit of joy, peace, and goodwill overlays the season. At no other time of year will shoppers be on their best behavior even while standing in long lines!

Christmas joy comes in many, often unexpected, ways. In giving and receiving. In sharing stories of other holiday seasons. In opening our hearts to the wonder of the season and passing that wonder on to others.

It is sometimes said that real joy is found by putting:

Jesus first
Others next
Yourself last.

May the joy that attended the birth of our Lord
fill your heart and life, not only during this holiday season,
but always.

Joy to the World!

Joy to the world,
The Lord is come!
Let earth receive her King;
Let every heart
Prepare Him room,
And heaven and nature sing,
And heaven and nature sing,
And heaven, and heaven,
And nature sing.

ISAAC WATTS (1674–1748)

ORIGIN OF THE HYMN

Isaac Watts, author of "Joy to the World!", is considered one of the greatest preachers of his time. In addition to his ministerial duties (including pastoring the Mark Lane Independent Chapel in London), he wrote numerous treatises, sermons, and books on topics ranging from teaching to psychology.

He also wrote more than seven hundred hymns. Many are still sung throughout the world, including "When I Survey the Wondrous Cross," often called the best hymn in the English language. Isaac Watts particularly loved the Psalms. The stirring charge to sing and rejoice found in Psalm 98 fired the prolific writer's imagination and became the inspiration for this treasured Christmas carol.

Wish of the Heart

Christmas Eve. Snowflakes joyously dancing in the air. Lighted windows. Chiming bells. Laughter.

The sound of carols interrupted Reverend Charles Blackstone's memories of happier Christmas Eves. The retired missionary opened his apartment door. A number of young people from a nearby church raised their voices in harmony. "Joy to the World!" "O Come, All Ye Faithful." "Silent Night." At last, "We Wish You a Merry Christmas," followed by the presentation of a garish net stocking, filled with the traditional orange, nuts, and hard candy that characterized such offerings.

Charles smiled. How many similar stockings had he passed out during his long career! "Thank you," he told the visitors. "God bless."

His impromptu concert-makers shouted back a variety of greetings before moving down the hall. Giggles again gave way to song.

Charles clutched the absurd stocking and slowly went back inside. He left the door ajar to catch the last sounds of the carols. His wife had died several years before. His only daughter, Alice, and her husband, Don, had been summoned to

Boston a week earlier. Don's father was seriously ill. Charles suspected Alice had been crying when she called to tell him the news.

"This is the first Christmas Eve we won't be together," she said. "But I can't let Don go alone. He and his father are as close as we are, Dad."

Charles hid his heaviness of spirit for Alice's sake. "I understand. You need to be with him. I'll be praying for all of you."

Now he switched on the television, a poor substitute for family and friends, but better than being alone. The first words he heard went straight to his heart.

"If you could have only one gift this Christmas, what would it be?" a game show host was asking a group of contestants. "What is the wish of your heart, the thing you long for above all else?"

Charles didn't wait for their answers. He shut off the program, sank into a comfortable chair and closed his eyes. He didn't need to consider the question. His deepest longing since poor health forced him to retire was simple and intangible.

"Lord," he said in a low voice, as he had done many times before. "The wish of my heart is and has always been the same: to know if my years as a minister were pleasing to You, and if I really made a difference. Will You one day say, ' Well done, good and faithful servant?' "

Someone tapped on the open door, then pushed it open. "Reverend Morris? Special delivery." The desk attendant held out a letter. "Merry Christmas!"

Charles eagerly took it. "And to you." As soon as she left, he opened it.

> *Dear Dad,*
> *Don's father is better, but we're staying on for a few days. We want you to have your Christmas present now, since we can't be there. Check your E-mail.*
>
> *Love, Alice and Don.*

What on earth was his daughter up to now? Charles hurried to his computer and did as she instructed. He gasped. There were over one hundred messages, from all over the world!

He was amazed that Alice had been able to contact so many people from such faraway places. Wanting to savor the pleasure, Charles hit the "print" button. He waited while page after page rolled out, then settled back in his chair.

The more he read, the bigger grew the lump in his throat. A boy he hadn't thought of for decades had never forgotten his pastor—how the preacher had put up bail when the boy had been falsely accused and arrested. A young woman saved from making a terrible mistake sent belated thanks. The widow of a man who vigorously opposed Charles on every church business matter shared how much her husband had respected his worthy opponent. On and on they went, each message filled with gratitude and thanks for their former minister's Christian example and practical service to his flock.

That night, Charles lay sleepless. Not because of the loneliness he had feared with Alice gone. Instead, he felt as if his room were filled with personalities. Faces filled with joy and happiness. At long last, Charles slept. Both his prayer and the wish of his heart had been granted.

May the wish of your heart
be granted this Christmas season.

I Heard the Bells
on Christmas Day

I heard the bells on Christmas day
Their old familiar carols play,
And wild and sweet the words repeat
Of peace on earth, good will to men.

Till, ringing, singing on its way,
The world revolved from night to day,
A voice, a chime, a chant sublime
Of peace on earth, good will to men!

HENRY WADSWORTH LONGFELLOW (1807–1882)

Serenade of the Bells

For ye shall go out with joy, and be led forth with peace:
the mountains and the hills shall break forth
before you into singing,
and all the trees of the field shall clap their hands.

ISAIAH 55:12

A touching legend tells of a young *señor* and *señorita* who lived in a small Mexican village. According to the story, they fell in love. As was the custom, they went to the mission church to make arrangements for a marriage. There they learned that the mission bells would need to ring in order for them to officially wed.

The young couple looked at one another in dismay. "It cannot be," the *señor* protested. "The bells have been broken for a very long time. What shall we do?"

"We must have faith," his *señorita* told him. "If our love is of *Dios* (God), He will send a miracle." She looked deep into her loved one's eyes. "I just hope it is soon."

During the days that followed, the *señor* became more and more discouraged. Why did a miracle not come when they

13

wanted it so badly? Surely the great love he felt for his *señorita* was pleasing to God.

"I will remain faithful all the days of my life," he vowed to the one he had chosen for his bride. "Should the marriage bells never ring, still I will love you."

"And I, you," she promised, her eyes wet with emotion.

That night, the village awakened in the dark hours. Great, rolling peals of music filled the air. Hastily donning clothing, the inhabitants raced outside. The mission bells sang their song, mighty and compelling. People for miles around hurried to the courtyard. No one was more joyful than the faithful *señor* and his *señorita*. The obstacle to their marriage had been overcome.

The next day, the young *señor* climbed up the bell tower to see how the bells that had been broken for years had rung out in the night. He looked, rubbed his eyes, and looked again. *The bells were still broken.*

He climbed down and, in hushed tones, told the villagers what he had discovered.

"We do not understand," the astonished people cried. "We heard the bells with our own ears. How can they still be broken?"

The oldest, wisest *señora* in the village hobbled over to the young couple. "Have you not heard that with love, nothing is impossible? Because of the love in these two hearts, even silent bells found their tongues and clamored for joy."

Jesus said unto him,
If thou canst believe, all things are possible.

MARK 9:23

May the deep, abiding love that
allows miracles to happen live in your heart.

Let Earth Receive Her King

FOR THE BEAUTY OF THE EARTH

For the beauty of the earth,
For the glory of the skies,
For the love which from our birth
Over and around us lies:
Lord of all, to Thee we raise
This our hymn of grateful praise.

For Thyself, best Gift Divine
To the world so freely given,
For that great, great love of Thine,
Peace on earth and joy in heaven:
Lord of all, to Thee we raise
This our hymn of grateful praise.

FOLLIOT S. PIERPOINT (1835–1917)

A Father's Gift

*If ye then. . .know how to give good gifts unto your children,
how much more shall your Father which is in heaven
give good things to them that ask him?*

MATTHEW 7:11

I closed my Bible and glanced out the window into winter beauty. Heavy, overnight frost had transformed ugly brown twigs and branches. Childish laughter echoed down the street, blending with the words I had just read.

My hands caressed the cover of the Bible now lying in my lap. Each year in early December, I begin making home and heart ready for Christmas. Preparations include reading the Christmas story from the second chapter of Luke and other favorite passages. What better way to "make room at the inn," than by reliving the actual, awe-inspiring events?

I closed my eyes in gratitude for the lovely morning, the matchless story I had just read, and for a special gift that went on giving.

While growing up, my brothers and I always received gifts jointly from Dad and Mom. Things changed the year I was seventeen. Dad announced that on Saturday morning our family would travel to the city closest to the small town where we lived. This in itself was a treat. There were huge chuck-holes in the road, and it took most of the day to make the one hundred mile round trip "down below."

The whole family usually knew the reason for our trip. Not this time. When we reached the city, Dad pulled into a parking space by a large stationery store. I asked, "What are we doing *here*?"

Dad's eyes twinkled, but he didn't answer until after the family trooped inside. Then he told me, "Pick out whatever Bible you want. It's my special gift to you."

I could scarcely believe my ears. Money was always tight in our family. We had a couple of worn Bibles, but this would be my very own. At last, I chose one in the King James translation. It had Jesus' words in bright red print and my name embossed in gold on the cover. I left the store feeling I had discovered gold.

The Bible went to church, youth camps, and rallies with me. Pages with my favorite verses became worn from Bible drills and study. The cover grew tattered. Years later, I had it recovered in leather, again with my name in gold.

Now I have a half-dozen other Bibles, sometimes used for

reference. But the one from Dad is my constant companion. It is a treasure chest of hope, comfort, inspiration, and more. A thousand memories are bound between its aging pages. Memories of home. Memories of family and friends and wonderful experiences. Memories of a loving father, who sacrificed a day of much-needed rest, in order to give me a priceless gift.

Now and then someone asks, "If disaster struck, what single thing would you most want to save, outside of persons or pets?"

My reply is always the same: the precious Bible Dad gave me one special Saturday nearly a half-century ago.

May you learn to recognize and cherish the precious gifts your heavenly Father bestows on you this Christmas and throughout the coming year.

Let Every Heart (even the smallest) Prepare Him Room

Perhaps there are no more notorious spoilers of the Christmas spirit than the cantankerous Scrooge and the mean-spirited Grinch. Each set out in an effort to douse the natural and radiant delight that accompanies the season. The miserly Scrooge spread his negativism equally among his family, office staff, and neighbors. The Grinch burgled the innocent Whoville, taking their Christmas ornaments, packages and trimmings. Despite their best efforts, however, neither the Grinch nor Scrooge could escape the highly contagious joy of the season.

After absconding with the Whos' Christmas loot, the Grinch is startled to hear celebratory singing rising from Whoville. The joyous Christmas spirit displayed by those who have nothing causes his heart to expand and teaches an important lesson.

Dr. Seuss captures this spirit beautifully in his "How the Grinch Stole Christmas." Seeing inhabitants of the village refuse to let anyone—even him—steal their holiday happiness, the Grinch recognizes that Christmas must be more than anything found in a store. Dr. Seuss further delights readers with

Whoville's firm belief their arch enemy's miniscule heart actually did grow three sizes that special Christmas day.

Ebenezer Scrooge's epiphany is just as dramatic. After his ghostly visitations, he finds and embraces the real meaning of the season.

> *Scrooge was better than his word. He did it all, and infinitely more. . . . He became as good a friend, as good a master, and as good a man, as the good old city knew. . . .*
>
> *Some people laughed to see the alteration in him, but he let them laugh. . . . His own heart laughed, and that was quite good enough for him. . .and it was always said of him, that he knew how to keep Christmas well, if any man alive possessed the knowledge.*
>
> *May that be truly said of us, and all of us! And so, as Tiny Tim observed, "God Bless Us, Every One!"*
>
> Excerpted from *A Christmas Carol,*
> by CHARLES DICKENS.

May your heart and spirit be touched with the transforming power of the season's joy.

And she brought forth her firstborn son,
and wrapped him in swaddling clothes,
and laid him in a manger;
because there was no room for them in the inn.

LUKE 2:7

Room in the Inn

Each Christmas, millions of persons around the world read the touching story of Joseph searching for shelter in an overcrowded Bethlehem. We share his sorrow and frustration at being unable to provide nothing better than stable space for his precious wife, Mary, and soon-to-be born child. And we can't help wondering about the innkeeper. Did his heart go out in compassion to the weary travelers? Or had he seen too many weary travelers to care? In any event, his response rings down through the ages, "*No room for you in the inn.*"

The story has another message: lost opportunities. It's fun to speculate about that incredible night. Suppose an innkeeper had given his own room and bed to the needy family. Would his establishment have later become the "Bethlehem Hilton," complete with sign, *The Messiah Slept Here*?

It is easy to believe we would have acted differently. Surely we would somehow have recognized the inherent greatness in what appeared to be an ordinary family. A nice thought, but highly unlikely. Every day of our lives, we play the role of innkeeper to both great and small. Do we "find room" in our hearts and busy lives to recognize and meet the needs presented to us?

A tiny girl trudges from person to person in a crowded room. She carries a book, looking for a welcoming lap and someone to read to her. Everyone is preoccupied. No one has time for her. So she sadly stands alone in the busyness that surrounds her, waiting and hoping for someone to make room for one small child and the book she clutches in her childish hands.

A teen stands at one side of a church foyer. Laughter, greetings, and talk of upcoming events swirl around her. A few people, including the pastor and his wife, seek her out. Their concern for her well-being warms her heart, but she wishes those her own age would take time to talk with her. She is too shy to approach the popular crowd without special invitation. If only they would call to her, "We're going to Burger King. You're coming, aren't you?" No one notices her. They are not intentionally cruel or uncaring, but the result is the same. There is no room for her in their midst—only on the sidelines.

A new family comes to town just before Christmas. We smile and welcome them to our church and neighborhood, but do we take time to discover their needs? Do they have work and a decent place to live? Do they have somewhere to go for Christmas? If not, is there room at our family celebrations for the strangers among us?

Jesus said, "Inasmuch as ye have done it unto one of the least of these my brethren, ye have done it unto me" (Matthew 25:40).

May God bless you as you make room in your life and heart for someone in need this holiday season.

The Blessings of Grace

Grace slumped dejectedly against the cold, barren wall. Her gaze traveled to the corner, falling on a tilting branch trying to pass itself off as a Christmas tree. *Who ever heard of decorating a pine limb?* When informed there would be no tree this year, the kids had dragged the downed branch from a local ditch, up-righted it in a tin bucket full of rocks, and christened it the "Baker family tree." The hanging snowflakes, cut from old newspapers collected along the road, didn't help the image.

Glancing across the room at her two sleeping children huddled together in blankets, Grace's frustration mounted. *We sleep on old mattresses on the floor. We eat whatever meager rations we can scrounge. It's been over a year since I could even buy them a new pair of shoes. Haven't we been through enough?*

Things had always been tight but livable. Between Jeff and herself, they'd made enough to pay for the rent on a moderate apartment, buy food and clothing for themselves and the kids, and have a little extra for gifts and the like. Two years ago, when Jeff left her and the kids, that all changed. Her minimum wage job and Jeff's sporadic-at-best child support payments, were stretched to the limit—and sometimes beyond.

Grace looked at the two presents set beneath the tree. She shuddered, thinking how disappointed the children would be to find two-liter soda bottles under the newspaper wrapping. Probably not as disappointed as finding out there wouldn't be a Christmas turkey. Somehow, she didn't think macaroni and cheese would get the same reception.

A light rapping on the door interrupted her dismal pity party. Standing in the cold night air was Bruce, the pastor from her local church. "Good evening, Grace. I was wondering if you could do me a favor?"

Grace was not in a "do unto others" mood, but courtesy dictated her response. "Of course. What do you need from me?"

"Well, Mrs. Goodson was supposed to deliver these care packages to needy families within our congregation, but she has become ill. I thought perhaps you might be willing to deliver them."

Deliver care packages for the needy? He must be joking. Has he looked around this place? Instead of expressing her thoughts, she nodded yes. The church had been there for her, after all. *What better way to usher in this fabulous Christmas, than watching others receive food and gifts we won't have this year,* her mind taunted sarcastically.

She watched silently as the pastor brought three large black plastic bags into the room. Each had a family's name designated on the tag. He thanked her, wished her a Merry Christmas, and was on his way. Staring at the bags, Grace couldn't help the bitterness coursing through her. *What am I going to tell my children? I'm not going to put them through watching people open gifts they can't have. I'll have to leave them with a neighbor when I make these deliveries.* Exhausted, she collapsed on her mattress.

Grace was roused by the sound of her children's excited voices. "Where did they come from? Do you think Santa brought them?"

Forcing her eyelids open, she observed her seven- and five-year-old daughters assaulting the gift bags. "Girls, please don't touch. Those aren't for us."

"Whose are they, Mom? Where did they come from?"

"Pastor Bruce brought them by and asked if I would deliver them to some families in our congregation."

"Can we come? Please?"

Looking at her children, Grace couldn't bear to say no. There had already been too many "nos" this Christmas. "Are you sure you want to come?"

Their smiling faces provided all the answers Grace needed.

The small family set out to deliver the first plastic bag marked Davis. Grace didn't know the Davises. As she followed the directions, she entered an upper-scale neighborhood and pulled in front of a large two-story house. "I must have the directions wrong," she muttered, glancing down to compare the addresses again. They matched. "I would give anything to have this house and yard.

I think they've switched who was supposed to deliver the care package to whom. She glanced in the rearview mirror at her children excitedly unbuckling their seat belts. *How am I going to explain this to them?*

With children in tow, she hauled the bag up the stairs. Her knock on the door was soon answered by a woman about her age. Grace couldn't help noticing the woman's questioning eyes were red and swollen. "I'm Grace Baker, and these are my children Dani and Emily. Pastor Bruce, from the church, asked us to drop this by."

"Thank you." The woman held out her hand. "I'm Carole. Won't you come in?"

Following her eager children, Grace glanced at the pictures lining the foyer. "Oh, I see you have a boy about Dani's age. What's his name?"

Carole's eyes filled with fresh tears. "It was John. He was

killed in a car crash last week."

Grace faltered, unsure of what to say. "Oh, I'm so sorry. I didn't know."

"He was our one and only. I miss him so much."

Grace visited with Carole and helped her unpack the food sent by the church. When it was time to leave, she promised she'd stop by after Christmas.

"Mom, I'm really glad we came." Emily said, climbing into the car. "She needed those presents so she wouldn't be so sad. I'm really glad we are going to be all together for Christmas."

"Me too, Honey." Grace looked at her children and suddenly felt blessed.

The next stop was at the Henderson place. Once again, Grace felt pangs of envy when gazing at the house and its surroundings. Widow Henderson took her time getting to the door. When she did appear, it was in her nightclothes.

"Mom, she's in her pajamas." Emily whispered loudly.

"You're right, young lady." Mrs. Henderson placed a frail hand on Emily's head. "I'm not feeling well today, and no one was here to help me out of my clothes." To Grace, she said, "The chemotherapy treatments just take it out of me— leave me feeling like an old woman." She winked and led them into the living room. Her delight at the packages and home-cooked meals shone on her face. "I'm so glad. I am too weak to cook anything these days. And what a blessing it is to have voices and laughter in my home. Having you come has been the greatest Christmas present I could have asked for. Please, promise you'll come again."

Grace assured her they would and then packed the girls into the car.

"Boy, Mom, I'm sure glad we brought her that food. She hadn't eaten in two days," Dani said. "It's no fun being sick and not getting anything to eat. I think she's really lonely, too."

"I think you're right." Grace responded. "I'm sure glad we're not sick and that we have each other—aren't you?"

The girls both nodded vigorously.

The car stopped in front of the last address, and Grace looked around. "I must have made a mistake," she mused, looking down at the paper. She shook her head in confusion. The curb numbers looked the same—but there was no house. She got out of the car and walked toward the stretch of beat-up lawn. A group of objects caught her eye. What were those? Tents? She approached cautiously and announced her presence. "Hello?" Halfway down the line of tents a flap opened, and a slight woman emerged.

"Hi. What can I do for you?"

"Um, well, we're looking for the Cameron house—do they live around here?"

The lady extended her bony arm and motioned toward the dirty tent. "I'm Ms. Cameron. Please come in."

Wide-eyed, Grace and her children ducked through the tent flap into a small area. Two tattered children sat playing on blankets. "I'm sorry I can't offer you a chair," Ms. Cameron continued. "But the blankets over there are clean." They sat down.

"Is this your house?" Emily asked unbelievingly.

"Yes. Well, at least until we have to move again. The neighbors only tolerate our tents so long before we're run off to another area of town. Sometimes we set up in a church parking lot, sometimes a park."

"How long have you lived like this?" Grace questioned.

"Since my husband was laid off six months ago. We were evicted for not paying our rent. Just try to get a new job without an address or phone number." She shook her head, her misery clearly evident. "During these winter months the shelters fill up. We had no choice."

Grace remembered the black plastic bag sitting outside the tent flap. She brought it through the doorway, and began extracting the contents. The Cameron children embraced the packages, opening them with wild abandon.

Clothing, blankets, toys and food soon lined the tent edges. The smiles that spread across the faces of the children, her own kids included, were wider than she had ever seen.

Ms. Cameron's tears fell freely. "Thank you so much. You have no idea how much this means."

Emily suddenly spoke. "Why don't you come to our house for Christmas? We have a tree with ornaments, and we're going to have macaroni and cheese. My mom's macaroni and cheese is the best in this world."

Emily's words warmed Grace's heart. "Yes, please come. We'd love for you to share our meal."

The Camerons agreed to be at the Baker house the next afternoon. Heading home, the girls discussed how this was the best Christmas ever, then fell asleep in the back seat. In the silence of the car, Grace contemplated the events of the day. *How could I have felt so down? How could I have overlooked my blessings? After today's visits, I feel like the luckiest woman on the face of the planet.* Grace looked up and sent a prayer heavenward.

Pulling to the curb in front of her house, Grace smiled and woke the girls. "Anyone up for a Christmas surprise?" She leaned against the car, laughing, as the girls rushed to the porch to open a very familiar black plastic bag with the name "Baker" on it.

May you remember and appreciate your simple blessings
this holiday season.

And Heaven and Nature Sing

SOUND OVER ALL WATERS

Sound over all waters, reach out from all lands,
The chorus of voices, the clasping of hands;
Sing hymns that were sung by the stars of the morn;
Sing songs of the angels when Jesus was born.

Blow bugles of battle, the marches of peace,
East, west, north and south, let the strong quarrel cease.
Sing songs of great joy that the angels began
Of Glory to God and of good will to man.

With glad jubilations, bring hope to the world;
The dark night is ending, and dawn has unfurled.
Rise, hope of the ages, arise like the sun;
All speech flow to music; all hearts beat as one!

JOHN GREENLEAF WHITTIER (1807–1892)

An Old-Fashioned Christmas

ADAPTED FROM *Little Women*

BY LOUISA MAY ALCOTT (1832–1888)

Scene 1

"Christmas won't be Christmas without any presents," grumbled Jo.

"It's so dreadful to be poor!" sighed Meg, looking down at her old dress.

"I don't think it's fair for some girls to have plenty of pretty things and other girls nothing at all," added little Amy, with an injured sniff.

"We've got father and mother and each other," said Beth contentedly.

The four young faces on which the firelight shone brightened at the cheerful words but darkened again as Jo said sadly, "We haven't got Father and shall not have him for a long time." She didn't say "perhaps never," but each silently added it, thinking of their father far away, where the fighting was.

"We've each got a dollar, and the army wouldn't be much helped by our giving that. Let's each buy what we want and have a little fun," cried Jo.

"I'll tell you what we'll do," said Beth. "Let's get Marmee

something for Christmas and not get anything for ourselves."

"Let her think we're getting things for ourselves, then surprise her," said Meg.

Scene 2

"Merry Christmas, daughters!" Marmee said. "Before we sit down to breakfast, I want to tell you about a poor woman with a newborn baby. Six children are huddled into one bed to keep from freezing. They have nothing to eat. My girls, will you give them your breakfast as a Christmas present?"

They were all unusually hungry, but Jo exclaimed impetuously, "I'm so glad you came before we began!" The others agreed. Assisted by their servant, Hannah, they gathered up cream, muffins, buckwheats, and firewood, then set out in the cold morning air.

"It is good angels come to us!" said the woman, when they reached her hovel.

"Funny angels in hoods and mittens," said Jo, and she set them laughing. Being called angels was very agreeable. There were not four merrier people in all the city than the hungry girls who gave away their breakfasts and contented themselves with bread and milk on Christmas morning.

"That's loving our neighbor better than ourselves, and I like it," said Meg.

The others did, too, and when Mrs. March opened her

presents, her joy more than repaid the girls for their sacrifices.

Scene 3
"Will the ladies walk down to supper?" Hannah said, after the exciting play Jo had written was presented to a dozen girls perched on the bed. When they reached the table, they rubbed their eyes and gasped. It was like Marmee to get up a little treat for them, but anything this fine was unheard of since the departed days of plenty. Pink ice cream. White ice cream. Cake. Fruit. French bonbons. And in the middle of the table, four great bouquets of hothouse flowers!

"Is it fairies?" asked Amy.

"It's Santa Claus," said Beth.

"Mother did it." Meg smiled her sweetest.

"Aunt March had a good fit and sent it," cried Jo in sudden inspiration.

"All wrong. Our neighbor, old Mr. Laurence, sent it," replied Mrs. March. "Hannah told one of his servants that you gave away your breakfast. Mr. Laurence is an odd old gentleman, but your unselfish act pleased him."

The girls learned Christmas joy comes through giving.
May your heart sing with gladness as you do
what you can to bring happiness to others.

And Heaven and Nature Sing

The angels mingled in the heavens,
awaiting Divine word.
Suppositions flew, and rumors passed.
Whose voice on high would be heard?

Would it be Gabriel?
He'd garnished the honor of announcing to Mary the news.
Or maybe Michael, the Archangel.
How would the Father choose?

Each angel longed to be the one
to declare the testament,
To tell the earth Christ had arrived:
The Gift Who was heaven-sent.

The Father appeared, and reverent silence
fell over the angel throngs.
He declared His great love
and expressed how pleased He was
with their beautiful songs.

"You know, I've been thinking," He told the large crowd.
"These tidings we celebrate
are the greatest the world will ever hear.
You all must participate."

A cheer raced through the crowd. The angels rejoiced.
Their joy they would get to declare.
With the shepherds abiding their flocks that night,
Each angel would also to be there.

And so on that eve, in Bethlehem fields,
The heavenly hosts God did send,
To praise his name, and proclaim his love,
and "peace, good will toward men."

JULIE REECE-DEMARCO (2001)

A Christmas Prayer for You

(BASED ON LUKE 1 AND 2; JOHN 1; MATTHEW 3)

I pray that you may experience the joy that came to Zacharias when the angel Gabriel told him, *"Thy prayer is heard. Thy wife Elisabeth shall bear thee a son. And thou shalt have joy and gladness."*

Mary, when Gabriel said unto her, *"Fear not. Thou hast found favour with God. Thou shalt conceive, bring forth a son, and call His name JESUS."*

Shepherds who heard a multitude of angels sing a song for all the ages, *"Glory to God in the highest, and on earth peace, good will toward men."*

Simeon and Anna in the temple, when they recognized Jesus as the promised One for Whom they had waited so long.

John, when he saw Jesus coming to be baptized and called out, *"Behold the Lamb of God, which taketh away the sin of the world."*

Most of all, I ask for you the joy that flowed from the Heavenly Father Who sent His Spirit in the form of a dove, saying, *"This is my beloved Son, in whom I am well pleased."*

Merry Christmas!